D

Do It Afraid!

Obeying God
in the
Face of
Fear

JOYCE MEYER

WARNER *Faith*®

NEW YORK   BOSTON   NASHVILLE

Unless otherwise indicated, all Scripture quotations are taken from *The Amplified Bible* (AMP). *Old Testament* copyright © 1965, 1987 by The Zondervan Corporation, Grand Rapids, Michigan. *New Testament* copyright © 1954, 1958, 1987 by The Lockman Foundation. Used by permission.

Scripture quotations marked (KJV) are taken from the *King James Version* of the Bible.

Warner Books Edition
Copyright © 1996 by Joyce Meyer
Life In The Word, Inc.
P.O. Box 655
Fenton, Missouri 63026
All rights reserved.

Warner Faith

Time Warner Book Group
1271 Avenue of the Americas, New York, NY 10020
Visit our Web site at www.twbookmark.com.

Warner Faith® and the Warner Faith logo are trademarks of Time Warner Book Group Inc.

Printed in the United States of America

First Warner Faith Edition: February 2003
10 9 8 7 6 5
ISBN: 0-446-69196-8 (Special Sales Edition)
LCCN: 2002115543

1

~~~~~

DO IT AFRAID!

*Obeying God
in the Face of Fear*

*H*as fear ever stopped you? Have you ever run away from something, disobeyed God or started something and then backed down because of fear?

If you have, you haven't been able to experience all the confidence available to you in God and the blessings He so desires to give to you. But you aren't alone.

Even though I'm a very bold person now, there was a time when I wasn't walking in the confidence and blessing God had for me. Over the years God has helped me understand how the bondages of fear took hold in my life, and He has showed me how to get out. In this book I explain what He taught me. I believe if you will open up your heart to receive as you read, you too will begin to walk free of the bondages of fear.

The Only Right Kind of Fear

There is only one right kind of fear described in the Bible—the reverential fear and awe of God.[1] Fearing God doesn't mean being afraid of Him or believing He is going to hurt you. Being afraid of God or what He might do is a perversion of the kind of fear God meant for you to have.

The fear of God the Bible talks about is the kind of fear we would have for anyone in authority. It is the kind of fear children should have for their parents, wives for their husbands, and students for their teachers. It is a type of godly respect that involves reverential fear and awe.

Of course, if you really look, you can see that Satan is doing a pretty good job of tearing down that whole structure. In our society there isn't a lot of respect for authority anymore. Instead, there is a lot of rebellion.

Proverbs 14:26 is an interesting Scripture: **In the reverent and worshipful fear of the Lord there is strong confidence.** Why? If you have a reverent and worshipful fear, you will obey. You will *do* what God says to do, and your confidence and trust in Him will continue to grow.

Having a reverential fear and awe of God has a positive effect on our relationships with other people. W. E. Vine says it "will inspire a constant carefulness in dealing with others in His fear."[2] Have you ever mistreated anybody? I know I used to be pretty hard to get along with. Sometimes I took my bad moods out on my kids or my husband, Dave.

I've noticed, however, the more reverential fear and awe I have of God and the more I realize Who God is, the more careful I am in my dealings with other people. I know I'm accountable to Him for my actions, and those other people are just as valuable to Him as I am.

The Wrong Kind of Fear

Without the reverential fear and awe of God, we quickly become people pleasers instead of God pleasers. Even though the Bible talks a lot about the fear of God, it never puts a stamp of approval on the fear of man. (See Proverbs 29:25.) And it doesn't put a stamp of approval on the fear of the devil either. You are to have *no fear* of the devil and *no fear* of man—what he thinks, what he says, what he does or what he might do.

The amount of turmoil which begins occurring in our lives when we become people pleasers instead of God pleasers is amazing. When we know that God is telling us to do something and we go do something else, we miss what God has planned for us. We are bowing our knee to man rather than to God. Then we have a gnawing feeling inside of us that puts us in a place of unrest. It steals our ability to have confidence.

How to Get Out from under the Control of Fear

Many people's lives are controlled by fear. The Greek word for fear is *phobos*. Initially it had the meaning of "flight." It "first had the meaning of flight, that which is caused by being scared; then, that which may cause flight."[3] In fact the words "fear" and "flight" are so closely connected that one meaning of "flight" is "a fleeing from or as from danger."[4] In other words, flight is what happened when fear came. Most people have a reason as to why they are afraid. Vine sums up those reasons by saying, "It seems best to understand it as that which is caused by the intimidation of adversaries."[5]

In some ways, I'm a very bold individual, but in other ways I also have bowed my knee to a spirit of fear. We all have areas in our lives in which we are pretty bold, but we might also have other areas in which we let fear overcome us as well.

Elisabeth Elliot, one of the wives of the five missionaries murdered by the Indian tribes in Ecuador to whom they were taking the gospel, along with Rachel Saint, the sister of one of the missionaries, evangelized the Indian tribes (including the very people) who killed their husband and brother. Elisabeth Elliot tells that at one time her life had been completely controlled by fear.

She wasn't free to do what she really wanted to do or what God wanted her to do because fear stopped her when she started to step out. A friend spoke three simple, but profound, words to her that set her free: "Do it afraid."

Fear Not

Whoever said we couldn't do it afraid? I can assure you it wasn't God. I have heard it said there are three hundred and sixty-five references to "fear not" in the Bible. I know there are at least three hundred and fifty-five, according to *Dake's Annotated Reference Bible,* one "fear not" for almost every day of the year.

Do you really want to obey the Scriptures and "fear not"? If so, you will be in good company because every person in the Bible who was ever used by God to any degree was told over and over by Him, "Fear not."

God Was with Joshua

One of those people was Joshua. Joshua, the man God chose to follow Moses, had a big job ahead of him: to lead the children of Israel into the Promised Land. He had plenty of opportunities to quit, but he didn't. He led the Israelites in taking the land, then ruled over Israel.

On one occasion God said to Joshua:

No man shall be able to stand before you all the days of your life. As I was with Moses, so I will be with you; I will not fail you or forsake you (JOSHUA 1:5).

We usually think this Scripture means God was saying to Joshua, "You go out and do what Moses did." I have interpreted it that way and have said, as I have heard other people say when teaching about this verse, "How would you like to have to go out and fill Moses' shoes?"

One day I saw something in this Scripture I had never seen before. God didn't say a thing to Joshua about going out and being like Moses or acting like Moses. The emphasis in this Scripture is on *God being with Joshua.* God said, . . . **As I was with Moses, so I will be with you.** God was telling Joshua that *He would be with him* just as He was with Moses.

God wasn't telling Joshua to be like Moses; but that He would be to Joshua what *He* had been to Moses. God would not fail or forsake Joshua. He was saying, "Fear not, Joshua, I will be with you!" (author's paraphrase). When God tells you He will be with you, that means no matter what the circumstances are like, everything will work out all right. That's a good reason to *do it afraid!*

If God wanted Joshua to go out and be like Moses, that interpretation of Joshua 1:5 puts us right back into the trap of thinking we have to be like somebody else. That isn't what God wants. God wants us to be ourselves so that we can fulfill the call He has placed on *our* lives. He will be with us. No matter what the circumstances are like, everything will work out all right because God will not fail or forsake us.

Joshua, because of his circumstances, had every reason to fall into fear, but God continued to encourage him and to let him know that He was with him. Look at what He said to him in Joshua 1:6, 7:

> Be strong (confident) and of good
> courage, for you shall cause this
> people to inherit the land which I
> swore to their fathers to give them. Only

you be strong and very courageous,
that you may do according to all the
law which Moses My servant
commanded you. Turn not from it to
the right hand or to the left, that you
may prosper wherever you go.

Then in verse 9 He goes on to say:

Have not I commanded you? Be
strong, vigorous, and very courageous.
Be not afraid, neither be dismayed, for
the Lord your God is with you
wherever you go.

When Joshua told the people what God had
told him, their response to him was one of obe-
dience. Even the people knew that if God would
just be with Joshua the way He had been with

Moses, everything would work out all right. So they answered Joshua and said:

> All you command us we will do, and
> wherever you send us we will go. As
> we hearkened to Moses in all things,
> so will we hearken to you; only may
> the Lord your God be with you as He
> was with Moses (VERSES 16, 17).

Think about this: If God gave these people all these instructions to fear not, don't you imagine they had something to fear? Surely they were facing some circumstances that didn't look good. Even though God had promised Joshua He would be with him, the Israelites still had to enter into the Promised Land of Canaan, where all of those giants were, and take the land city by city. They still had to fight their way through. But because God had already promised them victory, they could be confident.

God Was with Jeremiah

Now look at Jeremiah 1:5, 6:

> Before I formed you in the womb I knew
> and approved of you [as My chosen
> instrument], and before you were
> born I separated and set you apart,
> consecrating you; [and] I appointed
> you as a prophet to the nations.
>   Then said I, Ah, Lord God! Behold,
> I cannot speak, for I am only a youth.

We can see right away his problem is that he is looking at himself, not at God. But in verses 7–10 and 17 the Lord instructs him to not be afraid and promises to be with him.

But the Lord said to me, Say not, I am only a youth; for you shall go to all to whom I shall send you, and whatever I command you, you shall speak. Be not afraid of them [their faces], for I am with you to deliver you, says the Lord.

Then the Lord put forth His hand and touched my mouth. And the Lord said to me, Behold, I have put My words in your mouth. See, I have this day appointed you to the oversight of the nations and of the kingdoms to root out and pull down, to destroy and to overthrow, to build and to plant.

But you [Jeremiah], gird up your loins! Arise and tell them all that I command you. Do not be dismayed and break down at the sight of their faces, lest I confound you before them and permit you to be overcome.

In verse 19 the Lord warns Jeremiah that victory, however, will not come without a battle:

> And they shall fight against you, but
> they shall not [finally] prevail against
> you, for I am with you, says the Lord,
> to deliver you.

As God did with Joshua, He assures Jeremiah that He will be with him too.

God Was with Moses

Take a look now at what Moses said to the Israelites just after he led them out of the bondage of Egypt:

> When Pharaoh drew near, the
> Israelites looked up, and behold, the
> Egyptians were marching after them;
> and the Israelites were exceedingly
> frightened and cried out to the Lord.

And they said to Moses, Is it because there are no graves in Egypt that you have taken us away to die in the wilderness? Why have you treated us this way and brought us out of Egypt? Did we not tell you in Egypt, Let us alone; let us serve the Egyptians? For it would have been better for us to serve the Egyptians than to die in the wilderness. Moses told the people, Fear not; stand still (firm, confident, undismayed) and see the salvation of the Lord which He will work for you today. For the Egyptians you have seen today you shall never see again. The Lord will fight for you, and you shall hold your peace and remain at rest (EXODUS 14:10–14).

In other words Moses was telling the Israelites not to fall into fear even though the Egyptians were right behind them. He let them know in no uncertain terms the same God Who had delivered them out of Egypt would deliver them now. All they had to do was continue to place their trust in Him, and He would fight for them.

God Is with You

Now look at Philippians 1:28:

> And do not [for a moment] be frightened or intimidated in anything by your opponents and adversaries, for such [constancy and fearlessness] will be a clear sign (proof and a seal) to them [your enemies] of [their impending] destruction, but [a sure token and evidence] of your deliverance and salvation, and that from God.

In other words when trouble comes—and it will come—don't be intimidated by it. Psalm 34:19 says, **Many evils confront the [consistently] righteous, but the Lord delivers him out of them all.** Trouble will come, but you can be confident the Lord will deliver you from it—all of it. Instead of being intimidated by trouble, be constant and fearless. This will be a sign to your enemy that God is with you too.

The Bible Doesn't Say, "Don't Feel Afraid"

It is obvious from the four Scripture passages above there was something going on to *cause* the Israelites to *feel* afraid, and in each instance God said, "Fear not." If you are anything like me, when I hear the command to be fearless, right away I start thinking, "I'll try, but I can't help it. I don't want to feel afraid, but I can't help it."

What I want you to understand is that when the Bible says, "Fear not," it doesn't mean, "Don't *feel* fear."

Remember that any time you try to obey God, any time you try to step out into something you have never done before, any time you start trying to come out of a bondage you have worked yourself into, *fear* will rush right up in your face and try to stop you.

We think the problem is that we shouldn't feel this way. Feeling fear is not a problem! There isn't one thing wrong with you if you feel fear. The mistake you make is in bowing your knee to the feeling instead of going ahead and *doing* what you are afraid of *while* you are afraid.

Don't Run

Fear is nothing but a feeling which causes certain manifestations. It causes us to tremble, sweat, turn red, shake and our knees to wobble.

The Bible doesn't say, "Tremble not." The Bible doesn't say, "Sweat not," or, "Shake not." The Bible says, "Fear not." And the word *fear* implies running away from something! In other words God was telling them when *fear* comes, which it will because fear is the enemy of confidence, not to *let* it stop them. They were to *do* it afraid!

When I received this revelation, I could hardly believe it. It seemed too good to be true. I realized there wasn't anything wrong with me when my knees knocked together in new situations and sometimes I felt I was going to faint. Because I went ahead and did what I was supposed to do in spite of how I felt, I wasn't a coward. We are cowards only if we *run* because the word *"fear"* implies "flight"—"fleeing."

What God was telling Joshua and Jeremiah and Moses was, "I'm sending you out to do something, but I'm telling you ahead of time the devil will try to stop you with fear. Your enemies will come. You will *see* and *feel* things that will scare you. But, 'fear not.'" And "fear not" didn't mean, "Don't shake," "Don't sweat," "Don't tremble." "Fear not" meant, "Don't run"!

Don't Let Fear Determine
Your Destiny

Maybe you have been allowing a *feeling* to control and determine your destiny. Maybe you think that some people have fear and others don't. But the truth is that fear comes to *everybody*. What we do in spite of that fear makes the difference between victory or defeat in our lives.

If you will begin to act in spite of your fear, you will begin to get to the point of not even feeling fear. You will have gone through similar circumstances enough times to have developed some confidence in dealing with those types of circumstances. The things which used to frighten you won't frighten you anymore because you have some experience.

Any time you step out into something new, fear will try to stop you. Why? Because Satan is constantly trying to keep you from going forward. Once you have gained a certain amount of ground in an area, he will finally leave you alone and let you be there. But when you try to take one more step forward, that fear will rise up again.

One More Step Forward

I have had quite a bit of success in what God has called me to do, and all the glory goes to God because we are nothing without Him. Our part is to keep obeying Him and stepping out. When I look back, I can see what I have done is just dug in both heels and set my face like flint to do whatever God told me to do. I did it whether I was afraid or not.

If I shook, I did it. If I trembled, I did it. If I sweated, I did it. Whatever God said to do, I did it. And I can tell you with every step I took forward, I was *petrified*.

You might think I'm a brave sort of individual and not much would scare me. Generally that's true, but a few years ago I faced an opportunity I had never had before. I had an opportunity to minister in a meeting in Jacksonville, Florida, with other speakers who are known worldwide.

Sixteen hundred people were expected to show up at this conference, and really nobody was familiar with my ministry at the time. The only reason I had been invited to speak at the meeting was that my son, who was attending Bible college there, happened to live in the home

of one of the ladies on the board of the ministry
hosting the meeting. When he heard the board
was looking for one more workshop speaker, he
gave them my tapes on fear. They listened to
them, passed the tapes on to somebody else,
then invited me to come.

At the same time, I also received an invita-
tion to speak at a meeting in Colorado with a
very well-known speaker. "Finally," I thought to
myself, "my day has come!"

Because the meetings were back to back, we
had to go straight from Colorado to Florida without stopping at home to regroup between the
two. At the time, we were on around eight radio
stations, and I had traveled and ministered at
smaller meetings but never at a meeting this size.

When I arrived in Colorado, I found out the
big-name speaker had canceled, and I was left to
do all the meetings. I remember standing at the
window overlooking the parking lot of the

church waiting for all the people to show up. As it turned out, hardly anybody came to the meeting. Needless to say, ministering at that meeting was *really hard*. By the time I had finished, I was scared to even go to Jacksonville.

All kinds of thoughts began to race through my mind, "I will go down there, and nobody will even know who I am. All those other people will have full workshops, but nobody will come to my session. I'm going to feel like an absolute moron." The more I tried to put my thoughts aside, the more they seemed to persist.

Eventually, however, I did arrive in Jacksonville, Florida, and the conference. On the first night we were to get up and talk two or three minutes to describe what our workshop would be about. Usually I'm bold and don't have any trouble talking in front of a group, but this night was different. When I looked around, there were several hundred people in attendance, and the other speakers present were all lined up on the front row. Every one of them really well-known.

You have to understand, of course, that before this, people had been out at the tape table looking over my tapes. For whatever reason we were the only ones there with a tape table. Dave was at the table, and people were looking over the tapes saying, "Who is Joyce Meyer? Has anybody ever heard of her?" Some would even ask Dave, "Who is she?" And, of course, Dave would answer in a straight-faced way, "She is my wife!"

There I was in that Jacksonville conference looking at all those women after what I felt was a major defeat in Colorado. My confidence level wasn't too high, and even *I* was wondering what I was doing there. In other words, I was scared.

Nevertheless, I stood up to tell them what my workshop would be about. When I opened my mouth to say something, nothing came out! I was so scared I had lost my voice! You have to be pretty scared to lose your voice, and I was *pretty scared*. Then what was worse was the *topic* of my workshop *was* "fear"! So I swallowed, tried again, then went ahead and told them what my workshop would cover.

When I went to my hotel room that night I was still scared, but I didn't let it stop me. The next morning I got up and began to pray hard. Then I went out and sat on the balcony and cried. I said, "Oh, God, I'm so scared. What if I go up there and only four people decide to come? I'll have to go home with all those tapes we brought for that big table out there. Oh, God, I'm so scared!"

Dave was gone at the time. He had already left to set up the tape table. You may think people like me never get scared, but you don't know how many hotel rooms I've paced around before a meeting, wondering if anybody would come and if what I said would make any sense to anybody.

Eventually the time came for me to leave the hotel room, and I can remember walking down that long hall into the conference center wondering, "Will anybody come? God, what if nobody comes?" When I reached the center, the session began with a time of worship. Directly afterward we were released to go to our workshops.

In spite of my fears, God was faithful. The room was so full we could hardly move. Personally I think God did that just for me. I think He wanted to let me know He honored my faith because I was willing to "do it afraid."

When I finally finished preaching, the doors leading out of the meeting flew open, and those women literally mobbed the tape table. They were leaving with stacks of tapes so high they could hardly balance them. Dave was moving so fast he couldn't even think. He was just holding out his hand to collect the money. The women were saying, "I've never heard anything like this. Give me some of those tapes! I want a stack of them!"

We often go to Jacksonville, Florida, to minister now. I have more experience, and my confidence in God has increased to the point that those kinds of situations don't affect me quite the way they used to. But the first time was really tough. I went in there acting as though I knew what I was doing when inside I was saying, "Oh, God, what am I doing?" Even though I wanted to run, I didn't. I stayed and did it afraid!

Beneath the Fear

One of the biggest fears I have had to stand against all my life is the fear of making people mad. During my childhood, my dad expressed a lot of anger, and we never really knew what he was mad at. A lot of times he wasn't even mad at anybody. He was just mad, but he took it out on whoever was around.

Children tend to feel as though everything is their fault. I spent a lot of time in my life trying to figure out what I could do to keep him from getting mad. I used to be very careful all the time around him because I didn't want to upset him.

A few years ago God led me to discuss issues of my childhood with my parents. God had been working behind the scenes, and a miracle of restoration began taking place in my relationship with my parents! As a result, my parents released me to freely share the details of my childhood as I minister to help the people God has called me to help. My parents and I are now building a wonderful relationship! But to this very day, I really have to stand against a fear of making people mad. I have made some major strides forward in that area the last three years because I have come to the understanding that we just can't let people control us.

When Dave and I are driving somewhere, if he discovers he is driving in the wrong direction, he sometimes pulls into somebody's driveway in order to turn around and get resituated in the right direction. When he did this, though, I would get a panicky feeling and say, "What are you doing? What are you doing that for? Don't do that."

Then one day he looked at me and said, "What is your problem? I'm just trying to turn this car around." It was then that I began to ask God, "What is my problem?" God showed me I was afraid whoever lived in that house would come out ranting and raving like my dad might have done because someone was turning around in his driveway.

Let me share with you the second half of my revelation. As I really began to dig into this more,

I said, "Lord, what is it we are afraid of anyway?" The first thought that came to me was that we were afraid of man. But what does that amount to really? Beneath that, we are afraid of rejection. But that isn't even the end of it. What we are really afraid of, when all is said and done, isn't the devil. It isn't man. It isn't what people will think, say or do. What we are really afraid of beneath it all is *pain!* We just simply don't want to hurt.

I began to notice this tendency even in some of the most basic areas. For example, last winter when I left a building to go into the cold, I would clutch my coat around me and duck my head to try to keep from getting cold. But do you know what the Lord said to me one day? He just asked me a simple question, "Is any of this keeping you from being cold?"

When I thought about it for a second, I realized it wasn't. I was still cold! Plus I was putting myself under stress trying to keep from getting cold, ending up tense instead. What was I really trying to prevent? I was trying to prevent being uncomfortable. I was trying to protect myself.

But do you know what I have come to realize? We protect ourselves emotionally even more than we do physically! If somebody laughs at me, then I have emotional pain. If somebody gets angry at me, I have emotional pain. If somebody thinks I'm dumb, I have emotional pain. And what do we do? We try to protect ourselves emotionally.

Facing My Fear

When God was showing me this, we were in Maine. We had ministered there for a while and taken a couple of days off to stay at a bed and breakfast. It was a really nice home which had been refurbished and converted into a hotel.

Sandy and Danny, two of our vivacious, sanguine kids, were in the room next to us. While we were getting ready to leave, Sandy tripped and fell on top of her luggage rack. It crumpled and broke into pieces.

She took it downstairs to the people who owned the bed and breakfast and told them what had happened. They were very understanding and said, "Ah, well, that's all right. Never mind. They aren't very sturdy anyway."

Then about ten minutes later Danny came into our room, and *he* tripped and fell right on top of our luggage rack, breaking it into pieces. At times like those, you just want to leave, but we are people of integrity, so, of course, we wouldn't do that. So the only thing left to do was to go downstairs and tell the manager what had happened.

Normally I would have sent Dave to handle a situation like that because handling those kinds of incidents doesn't bother him at all. He just goes and does it, as simple as that. I, on the other hand, wouldn't have gone down there and talked to that manager for anything. Fear would have stopped me. But because I had just received this revelation about fear, I knew God wanted me to be the one to talk to the manager.

I began to think it out, "Now I'm going to go down there to talk to the manager, and all I'm going to get is a little pain. I've experienced pain in the past. Surely I can survive this pain. I mean, what is the worst that could happen? He could get mad. Okay, so what if he gets mad and says, 'What? You broke another luggage rack!' Or what if he laughs or thinks we are ridiculous or makes a false accusation? How many things could he possibly do?" Of course, all of them would have amounted to emotional pain. Right? Sometimes the *fear* of doing something is much worse than doing it, and the fear of it torments you much more than the actual doing of it. When you finally go and get it done you find, there isn't much to it. This time I knew that God just wanted me to go do it afraid.

I picked up the broken luggage rack and walked downstairs to the manager. I said, "Ah, do you know my daughter? Well, just a little bit ago she broke a luggage rack." The manager looked at me and said, "Yeah, I already know about that."

I went on, "No, you don't understand. This is another one. My son fell on top of this one." This time I had her attention, and she said, "I can handle one, but two? I don't know." Danny was standing there beside me, so she turned to him and said, "Are you trying to sit on these?"

Quickly I answered, "No, ma'am, he didn't try to sit on it. My daughter fell on top of one, and my son fell on top of the other one. How about if I pay for them? Just tell me what they cost, and I'll pay you for them." Do you know that in just a few seconds, the whole thing was over, and we went on about our business.

Walking through
Doorways of Pain

If you keep letting fear rule your life, you are never going to feel good about yourself. At some point, you have to face your fear and come out of the bondage in which it has held you. Sometimes you don't even know exactly how you got into that bondage. All you know is that you are afraid. Oftentimes it relates to things which happened to you in your past. But God can bring you out of that fear if you will only trust Him.

In order to illustrate how we can find a way out of our bondages, God gave me an illustration involving doors. For an example let's look at my fear about making people mad at me. I had that fear primarily because of traumatic events in my life which led me into that particular bondage.

God showed me that we go through door-ways of pain to get into bondage. For a better picture of this, imagine me, as I walk along in life, one day encountering somebody who gets mad at me. As a result, I'm wounded emotion-ally. Then the next day somebody rejects me, and I experience pain from that. Painful experi-ences like those continue to happen day in and day out. Eventually I say to myself, "I don't want that to happen anymore." I start trying to protect myself by erecting emotional doors I can slam shut any time the pain gets to be too much. So now what happens?

I experience pain. I remember the door I have erected and decide to hide. So I walk through that doorway and slam the door shut. I feel a tinge of relief and go on with life.

I got up my nerve and opened the door to McDonald's. In the back of my mind, I'm thinking, "How will they know I just came in for some water. Maybe they'll think I've been eating here all along and just came up to the counter to ask for some water."

But as soon as I walked through the door, the lady at the counter looked directly at me. Then I thought to myself, "That blew that. Now she knows I'm coming in fresh from the outside just for water." So do you know what I did? I turned my body and started to walk toward the bathroom. I had decided to stay in the bathroom awhile, then come out to get my water later. Maybe by then a different person would be at the counter.

Halfway down the hall I thought, "What are you doing? Go out there and get your water!" I turned around, marched down the hall, up to

Then something else happens, so I erect another doorway and go through it. Now I'm back here behind two layers of bondage, and I'm saying, "Man, I'm going to protect myself from all this. I don't want any more of that pain."

Then every time a similar situation comes up, the enemy will remind me of that pain. He will loom up in front of me and say, "Do you remember when that happened and how you felt? Well, it is going to happen again." Immediately you say, "I don't want any more of that because it hurts too much." Then you go through more things in your life, and you find yourself behind more and more doors, getting into more and more bondage.

You don't exactly sit down and think this out, but that is exactly what is happening. You had to go through pain in order to get into bondage. In order to get free from the bondage, you will have to go back through the same doors of pain. But this time instead of going deeper *into* bondage, you will be coming *out* of bondage.

The way you will come out will be through similar circumstances set up for you. They won't be the same set of circumstances, but they will remind you of the previous circumstances. This time when they come up, however, you will respond differently to them. You will face your fear, you will face your pain, and you will walk through the situation this time going the opposite direction, toward freedom.

Facing My Pain

Let me share with you an example of this happening in my life. My daughter and I had eaten out midday because I had an appointment in the afternoon. Later when we were out, I was thirsty and just wanted some ice water.

Every now and then I will order a s[...] not very often because I like water. Som[...] we go into McDonald's just for water. Sir[...] spend a lot of money at McDonald's on[...] and fast-food, we feel it's fine to do that. [...] ally, *we* don't go. We usually send Dave bec[...] he doesn't mind.

I don't know about you, but I have alw[...] felt funny going into a restaurant and aski[...] "May I use your bathroom?" or "May I have fo[...] cups of water?" especially if I'm not eating ther[...] I assume they will think I'm really stupid to as[...] for water without buying anything.

Because I made the decision to do things afraid no matter how I felt, I decided to not be held in bondage anymore. I'm a grown woman. If I want to go to McDonald's to get a cup of water, I ought to be able to. If people don't like it, they can think what they want. Their reaction won't bother me because I have decided to do it.

the counter and said, "I would like two cups of water, please, with lots of ice." After the lady handed them to me, I turned around and walked out the same doors I had come in. I was so proud of myself. I was an overcomer. I had asked for a cup of water at McDonald's! I did it afraid!

Really though, it wasn't the idea of asking for a cup of water that I was struggling with. It was that old pain from way back that kept saying, "What if they get mad? Then what are you going to do?" But regardless of what I thought or how I felt, I had decided to go back through that doorway of pain.

I may have had a little fear and a little trembling. I may have felt my heart beating a little faster than normal. But the Bible doesn't say, "Tremble not." It doesn't say, "Sweat not." It just says, "Fear not!" So, charge, I went back through the doorway.

How to Get Free from Bondages

As I did things I was afraid to do over and over again, I became more and more free. If you are looking for an easier way to do this, you won't be able to find it. There is no other way out except *through*. And how are you going to do it? You will do it afraid.

If you are waiting for a time in your life when you don't feel any fear, you will be waiting until Jesus comes because fear will *always* be there to stop you. You just have to make up your mind ahead of time that when that situation comes around again, you are going to do it afraid.

Look at Hebrews 10:35, 38:

Do not, therefore, fling away your fearless confidence, for it carries a great
and a glorious compensation of
reward.

But the just shall live by faith [My righteous servant shall live by his conviction respecting man's relation-ship to God and divine things, and holy fervor born of faith and cojoined with it]; and if he draws back and shrinks in fear, My soul has no delight or pleasure in him.

This Scripture doesn't say, "If he feels fear." To me it is saying, "If he draws back and shrinks away from the challenge in front of him."

God said to Joshua, "Fear not." He said to Jeremiah, "Fear not." He said to the Israelites through Moses, "Fear not." What He was saying to them was that fear *will* come. And when it comes, you may shake, you may tremble, you may sweat, your heart may beat hard, your knees may feel as though they are about to buckle. He was asking them, though, to put their confidence in Him, to believe He was with them and to not run.

Face Your Fears

You may be someone who is being stopped by fear. All your life God has been speaking things to you, but instead of obeying God, you have drawn back in fear of what may happen or of what people may say or do. As a result, your life is a confused mess. You aren't happy because you know you aren't fulfilling the will of God for your life.

You may be so bound, you are even afraid to go forward at a meeting to allow the Spirit of God to minister to you, so you leave the meeting still bound by your fears. You may want to confront certain issues in your life, but you never do because you are afraid. You just keep sweeping the issues under the rug and letting fear control you. You may try to rationalize your way out of it, but deep down you know that what you are doing is destroying it.

Just Do It!

First Peter 5:8 (KJV) says, the devil, as a roaring lion, walketh about, seeking whom he *may* devour. Notice the Scripture says "may" and not "will." In other words, you have something to do with whether he is able to devour you. And if you know anything about Satan, he doesn't have any power. The only power he has is the power you give him. Fear, of course, is one of his favorite tactics, so he will try to use fear to stop you. But don't give in to him. Go ahead and do it afraid.

When God tells you to give somebody a tract or witness to a person, say, "Yes, Lord, I want to do what You're telling me to do. I feel kind of afraid, Lord, but I believe You're with me, so I'm just going to do it. And, devil, you can just forget the plans you had for me because I know Who God is, and you don't scare me. I'm going to do what God told me to do."

When God tells you to give an extra big offering in church because He wants you to plant it as a seed (Luke 6:38) so that you can come up higher in your finances, say, "Okay, Lord, I'll do it. I know that means I will have to really trust You for some provision, but because I believe I'm hearing from You, I'll do it. Yes, Sir, I'll do it. And, devil, you can forget trying to scare me away from doing it. I've heard from God. I'm going to do what God said. I don't care if I shake, tremble or sweat. I will do it, afraid or not."

Don't let the devil rob you of the destiny God has for you. Step out and face your fears; face your pain. Go ahead and shake, tremble and sweat. God didn't say not to feel fear—He said not to run! You can be a victorious Christian, or you can be one who is never quite able to enjoy the fullness of God. The only difference between the two is that one is stopped by fear and the other does it afraid. Determine today to *do it afraid!*

ENDNOTES

1. James Strong, *Strong's Exhaustive Concordance of the Bible* (Nashville: Abingdon, 1990), "Hebrew and Chaldee Dictionary" p. 52, #3372, 3373 "to revere"; "Greek Dictionary of the New Testament" p. 76, #5399 "to be in awe of, i.e., *revere.*"

2. W. E. Vine, *An Expository Dictionary of New Testament Words* (Revell: Old Tappan, New Jersey, 1940), Vol. I, p. 84.

3. Ibid.

4. *Webster's New World College Dictionary,* 3rd ed., s. v. "flight."

5. Vine, Vol. I, p. 84.

JOYCE MEYER has been teaching the Word of God since 1976 and in full-time ministry since 1980. She is the bestselling author of more than seventy inspirational books, including *Approval Addiction*, *In Pursuit of Peace*, *How to Hear from God*, and *Battlefield of the Mind*. She has also released thousands of audio teachings as well as a complete video library. Joyce's *Enjoying Everyday Life*® radio and television programs are broadcast around the world, and she travels extensively conducting conferences. Joyce and her husband, Dave, are the parents of four grown children and make their home in St. Louis, Missouri.

To contact the author write:

Joyce Meyer Ministries
P. O. Box 655
Fenton, Missouri 63026
or call: (636) 349-0303

Internet Address: www.joycemeyer.org

Please include your testimony or help received from this book when you write. Your prayer requests are welcome.

To contact the author
in Canada, please write:
Joyce Meyer Ministries Canada, Inc.
Lambeth Box 1300
London, ON N6P 1T5
or call: (636) 349-0303

In Australia, please write:
Joyce Meyer Ministries—Australia
Locked Bag 77
Mansfield Delivery Centre
Queensland 4122
or call: (07) 3349 1200

In England, please write:
Joyce Meyer Ministries
P. O. Box 1549
Windsor
SL4 1GT

or call: (0) 1753 831102

* Study Guide available for this title